DOCKSIDE

STAGE
5

BOOK 2

SO FUNNY

Philippa Bateman

RISING STARS

"What are you doing?" asked JJ.
"You can see what I'm doing! I'm putting rubbish in the bin," said Tasha.
"I'll hold the lid up for you," said JJ.

"What is the matter with you?" asked Tasha. "You never offer to help me."

"Just be happy that I'm helping you now," said JJ as he slammed the bin lid shut.

"That yellow T-shirt looks good on you," he added as Tasha walked away.

"You're being too nice, JJ. You'd better not be up to any tricks," Tasha joked.

"Tricks? Like these?" laughed JJ as he whizzed past her on his skateboard. "He's amazing on that thing," thought Tasha, but there was no way she was telling him that!

"Where are you off to?" JJ asked.
"Just hanging out with the girls
at the coffee shop," she replied.

"Will your new friend from Poland be there?" JJ asked.

"Anna?" asked Tasha.

"Yes. Anna. I saw you with her at Club OK," said JJ.

"Yes, she'll be with us," said Tasha.

"I'll come with you," said JJ.

Suddenly Tasha knew what JJ was up to. "You like Anna! You want a date with Anna!" teased Tasha.

"OK, I admit it! I like Anna. Don't gossip about it, OK?" hissed JJ, getting redder by the second.

14

"OK, you can come with me. But if you want Anna to like you, smile and be funny. And fix your hair!" said Tasha. JJ started gelling his hair.

JJ asked Tasha what else he should do to impress Anna.
"Show her some of your skateboard skills! But no bragging," giggled Tasha.

Anna came up to JJ and Tasha in the car park of the coffee shop. They chatted about skateboarding.

"I can do an Ollie and a back-flip," he bragged.
"An *Ollie*? A *back-flip*? What is this?" asked Anna.
"I'll show you," said JJ.

JJ jumped on his skateboard and started twisting and turning on a narrow ramp. Then he landed ... flat on his back!
He just missed hitting Anna as he fell into a rubbish bin.